IMAGES
of England

BRIDGWATER
THE SECOND SELECTION

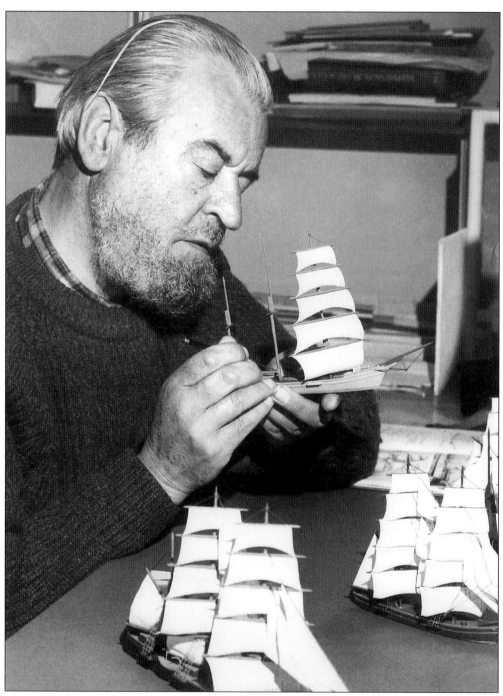

Museum Custodian, John St John Earl, 1979. Since Bridgwater Town Council opened Blake Museum in 1926, it has grown into the museum of local history and archaeology for Bridgwater and the surrounding area. In 1974 the museum's management was taken over by Sedgemoor District Council, and Mr St John Earl was appointed Museum Custodian, from 1975 to around 1985. (79186-2)

IMAGES
of England

BRIDGWATER
THE SECOND SELECTION

Compiled from
the collections at Blake Museum

TEMPUS

First published 2001
Copyright © Sedgemoor District Council, 2001

Tempus Publishing Limited
The Mill, Brimscombe Port,
Stroud, Gloucestershire, GL5 2QG

ISBN 0 7524 2444 0

Typesetting and origination by
Tempus Publishing Limited
Printed in Great Britain by
Midway Colour Print, Wiltshire

Proceeds from the sale of this book will contribute to the continued development
and care of the photographic collections at Blake Museum, Bridgwater.

Bringing home the harvest, alongside the Taunton and Bridgwater Canal, c. 1949. The
photographs included in this selection illustrate a period in the twentieth century when much
was about to change; in both town and countryside. (444)

Contents

Acknowledgements

The illustrations in this book have been selected from the photographic collection of Blake Museum, many of which have been given or loaned to the Museum over the years. Particular thanks go to the family of Don Smith, who kindly donated the Douglas Allen Photographic Studio collection of photographs to the Museum in 1999, and to Douglas and Margaret Allen, David Williams and Roger Brown who have helped with the identification of some of the photographs. We must also thank the many visitors to the museum who have added additional information to the photograph captions.

We would also like to thank the local people who appear in these photographs. Whilst it has not been possible to trace all of the subjects, we hope that they enjoy sharing their happy memories with others.

And finally, thanks must go to the members of the museum team who have researched and compiled this book, Carolyn Cudbill, Sarah Harbige and David Sebborn.

Introduction

This is the second selection of photographs to be chosen from the collection at Blake Museum. Since 1998, when the first selection was published, the collection has grown at an incredible rate. Perhaps the most important addition has come from the former Douglas Allen Photographic Studios in St John Street, Bridgwater. This collection of between 15,000 and 20,000 negatives and prints is slowly being catalogued and researched, and forms the core of the photographs selected for this volume.

Douglas Allen established his studio at No. 7 Friarn Street, Bridgwater in 1948. The studio became well known for its commercial, industrial, and public relations work and served a wide list of clients across the South West. Mr Allen also took photographs of a more personal nature, family groups and special events such as weddings, birthdays and anniversaries. The studio family portrait became instantly popular with the invention of photography in the mid-nineteenth century, and continues to be a mainstay of photographic studios today.

Douglas Allen also produced photographs for the several newspapers across the county, including the *Bridgwater Mercury*. He was paid 15s a week for a photograph to illustrate a news item or special event in the town. By the 1950s local newspapers had begun to use more photographs, but far less than we see today.

In 1952 a small studio and darkroom was set up, with the co-operation of Dosson Bros. in the High Street, and a receptionist was employed. As the business grew, an assistant, Donald Smith, joined the firm. Mr Smith was a fifth-generation photographer, who after completing his National Service, returned to his family's photographic business in Axminster. He moved to Somerset in 1958 to gain more experience and later became a partner in the firm. In 1960 the studio moved to new premises in St John Street and when Mr Allen retired, in around 1985, Mr Smith bought the business and continued to trade under the Douglas Allen name.

After Don Smith's death, the business was sold in 1999. Another industrial photographer purchased the industrial work and collection and the studio building was converted into flats.

The photographs that are now in the care of Blake Museum are largely from the early period of the studio's life, with most having been taken from around 1954 to 1960. They reflect not only the work of an important regional photographic studio at that time, but also how society and familiar landmarks were changing in the mid-twentieth century. The images selected for this publication look at everyday experiences – at school, work and shopping, and special occasions like weddings, anniversaries and birthdays. They also look at what was happening in the cultural and sporting life of the town, the enthusiastic amateur dramatic scene, the carnival and skittles teams, as well as what was changing in the surrounding area. Perhaps the most dramatic changes are in the buildings that have gone or changed, but there have also been changes in the countryside, and in the way we grow and buy our food.

This collection hopefully reflects those changes, of the past fifty years, and the people who experienced them. We hope you enjoy this second volume of photographs to come from the museum – which only begins to scratch the surface of the history of this fascinating town.

Sarah Harbige
September 2001

Fore Street and West Quay, Bridgwater, c. 1960. This view was taken from the YMCA building at the junction of East Quay and Salmon Parade and shows the roof tops towards King Square. The Punch Bowl Inn at No. 2 Fore Street closed in 1964.

One
The Changing Townscape

The George Williams YMCA Memorial Hall, Bridgwater, 1965. Erected in 1887 on the corner of Eastover and Salmon Parade, it was one of the finest landmarks in old Bridgwater. It was demolished in 1968 and replaced by a modern shop. (65152)

Demolition of the corner of Fore Street and Binford Place, Bridgwater, August 1966. A view of the building site from King Street towards Salmon Parade and the YMCA. (V187-1)

Town Bridge and Fore Street, Bridgwater, c. 1950. In Binford Place, to the left in this photograph, there was a range of eighteenth and nineteenth-century buildings with modest shop fronts. (557)

Binford Place, Bridgwater, *c*. 1965. This atmospheric view of Binford Place was taken at high tide. It says more about the photographer's art than the newly built shops and flats. (V192)

Farmer's Corner, Bridgwater, 1957. This familiar and picturesque landmark of old Bridgwater stood at the junction of Monmouth Street and St John's Street. It was demolished to provide greater visibility at the road junction and is now the site of a private car park. (V34-1)

Fore Street Congregational chapel, Bridgwater. The chapel was built in 1862. (V41a)

Demolition of Fore Street Congregational chapel, 1964. Like so many other nineteenth-century buildings in the centre of the town, it was replaced by nondescript modern shops. (V101)

Construction of the head offices for the Bridgwater Building Society (looking from Northgate), King Square, Bridgwater, February 1962. (V69-1)

King Square, Bridgwater, c. 1978. The headquarters of the Bridgwater Building Society blend in with its older neighbours. From 1988 the building housed the main offices of Sedgemoor District Council. (V587.)

Demolition of Starkey, Knight & Ford Brewery, Northgate, Bridgwater. This was the last working brewery in the town, and it closed in 1964. (V178-1)

North Street, Bridgwater in the 1950s. The cottages on the right-hand side were demolished in 1962. On the junction of North Street and Penel Orlieu, they were to be replaced by Westgate House, occupied by the Inland Revenue and a motor car showroom. (Photographic Collection, North Street U)

The Bridgwater Courts, c. 1937. Bridgwater had substantial areas of rundown Victorian working-class housing in the Clare Street and Market Street area and around West Street and Albert Street. Living conditions were regarded as harsh and the responsible authorities had been carrying out a campaign since before the Second World War to have these areas demolished. (Photographic Collection, 1989/87)

Demolition of West Street, Bridgwater. The Victorian cottages of Albert Street at the rear of the site were also soon to be demolished. (GP401)

West Street, Bridgwater, July 1977. The new flats, which replaced the Victorian courts and alleys, were infinitely better appointed, but the community spirit of the area had gone. (V417)

The old and the new, West Street, Bridgwater, c. 1969. Boarded-up houses await demolition alongside the new tower block. (V138-1)

Theatre Place and Clare Street, Bridgwater, *c.* 1958-1960. The site was demolished to make way for a car park. (V415)

Friarn Street, Bridgwater, 1963. The buildings on the left were demolished to make way for the Broadway. On the right-hand side is the rear of Winkworth's Garage. (63130-4)

The site of the new Broadway, Bridgwater, *c.* 1957-58. Traffic congestion in the town made it imperative that a bypass to the town centre should be built. The construction of the Broadway in 1958 not only altered the road layout of the town, but also resulted in the demolition of Holy Trinity church in Taunton Road; seen here to the right in the photograph. The last church service was held in 1958 before it was re-located to a new housing estate at Hamp. (V76-3)

Monmouth Street, Bridgwater, *c.* 1957. The Queen's Head Hotel, at the junction of Monmouth Street with Eastover (on the right) and St John's Street (on the left), was demolished to provide the eastern end of the new Broadway in 1958. (V16a)

Construction of Blake Bridge, Bridgwater, 1957. The second road bridge, built in the town across the River Parrett, provided four carriageways. However, increasing volumes of traffic have made it necessary to build more bridges. (59144)

Broadway, Bridgwater, c. 1960. Opened on 28 March 1958, the Broadway was the first of a number of road schemes designed to take pressure away from the centre of the town. In the background is the newly constructed technical college. This too was to become unable to meet demand and was replaced by a new college complex at Bath Road. The buildings are now owned by a health trust. (V83)

19

West Quay, Bridgwater. Mercifully, the character of some parts of Bridgwater have been preserved. West Quay retains much of its former charm, notwithstanding some redevelopment at the end of Chandos Street, to the right in the photograph. (V563)

Two
Open for Business

Counter service at David Greig, No. 40 Fore Street, Bridgwater, 1960. By the late 1950s many of the country's traditional grocery stores were adapting to welcome the new trend for self-service. Supermarkets had arrived and high streets across the country were beginning to see a marked change. (60105a)

Co-op, King Street, Bridgwater. The Co-operative movement began in Rochdale in the late nineteenth century and soon spread countrywide. Buying in bulk from suppliers, they were able to pass on benefits to their customers in the form of a dividend. There were Co-op branches throughout the town, but King Street was home to the central offices and a grocery department. (V472)

Boots the Chemist, Nos 34-36 Fore Street, Bridgwater, November 1954. Born in 1850, Jesse Boot took over his family's shop in Nottingham in 1877, and by 1896 he owned sixty shops in twenty-eight towns. (54365)

L.H. Llewellyn Ltd, Chemist, No. 15 Penel Orlieu, Bridgwater. (GP101)

Fore Street, Bridgwater in the 1950s. At No. 13 Lennards Ltd, Shoe Shop, at No. 15 Phillips & Co., Tailors, Drapers and Milliners and at No. 17 Basker & Co., Chemists. (V11)

Numbers 24-28 Fore Street, Bridgwater in the 1950s. Maynards Tobacconist and Confectionery shop had moved across the road to No. 21 by 1962. In 1953 Bridgwater's Freeman, Hardy and Willis store was just one of 500 shoe shops in the countrywide Sears' chain. (GP1)

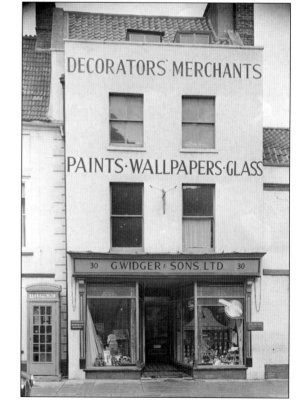

G. Widger & Sons Ltd, Decorators' Merchants, No. 30 High Street, Bridgwater, November 1954. Located next to the Mansion House this building was demolished by mid-1965 and replaced with a modern structure. (54366a)

Marks & Spencer, Nos 19-20 Cornhill, Bridgwater. Founded by Michael Marks in Leeds in 1884, the company began life as a market stall, selling goods at a fixed price of a penny. In 1890 Tom Spencer joined the company, which continued to grow. The *St Michael* brand was introduced in 1924. The Bridgwater branch of the store closed in February 1990. (Photographic Collection, Cornhill U)

Marks and Spencer, Nos 19-20 Cornhill, Bridgwater, clothing sales area, August 1957. (57335b)

Hodges & Sons (Clothiers) Ltd, No. 12 Cornhill, Bridgwater, September 1959. The Bridgwater Chamber of Trade often organized window display competitions and firms liked to have their efforts photographed. (59313)

Dosson Brothers Ltd, Independent Outfitters, Nos 45-47 High Street, Bridgwater, May 1954. This window display was entered in competition for a manufacturer's prize, for Aertex. (54209a)

Worlds Stores Ltd, No. 8 Fore Street, Bridgwater, September 1959. Another new self-service grocery store for the town. Workmen at the first floor window may show that the store has only recently opened. (59303a)

Lipton Ltd, No. 7 Fore Street, Bridgwater. Founded by Sir Thomas Lipton in Glasgow in 1871, the company grew into one of the major multiple grocery chains. Like many grocers they concentrated on tea, dairy products and cold meats, selling at fixed prices and trading on a cash-only basis to keep overheads low. (Photographic Collection, Fore Street U)

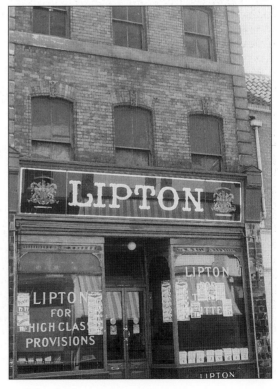

David Greig, No. 40 Fore Street, Bridgwater, 1960. Greig's were part of a national chain of grocery and provisions stores. This store continued with the traditional way of service, in competition with the growing number self-service supermarkets in the town. (60105b)

David Greig, No. 40 Fore Street, Bridgwater, 20 October 1960. In 1960 the manager was John Botfield. (Photographic Collection, 1997/90/2)

Home and Colonial Stores, No. 3 Eastover, Bridgwater, November 1959. This photograph may have been commissioned for the opening of this new self-service grocery store, which opened in 1959. The introduction of self-service was advertised in the *Bridgwater Mercury* on 1 December 1959 as follows: 'Prices are clearly marked and everything is displayed for your convenience – under the latest and most hygienic conditions. Simply select the goods you require and pay as you leave. What could be easier?' (59380a)

F.W. Woolworth & Co., No. 27 Eastover, Bridgwater, July 1956. Frank Winfield Woolworth was born in New York state in 1852. His retail empire was based on the 5 and 10 cent stores he first opened in the United States in 1879. His first English stores opened in 1909 and sold everything for a fixed price, 3d or 6d. However, by 1935, the company had dropped this idea in favour of self-service stores. Within a few years of this photograph being taken, the Bridgwater branch of Woolworth's had moved across the road and was replaced by a self-service supermarket. (56312)

International Stores, No. 27 Eastover, Bridgwater, June 1959. The International Tea Company developed as a multiple grocer in much the same way as Liptons and Home and Colonial Stores, which both had branches in the town. The first response to self-service from the British public was not very enthusiastic, many were not keen to 'help themselves' and worried that other customers would see their purchases through the wire baskets. (59232a)

Opening day at International Stores, No. 27 Eastover, Bridgwater, 5 June 1959. The town's first big self-service store opened in what was the former home of Woolworth's. It had 2,000 square feet of shopping space and carried 2,000 lines of goods. Special guest, actress Gwen Berryman, better known as Doris Archer, opened the store and signed autographs. (59232b)

Three
At Work

Excavating clay at Colthurst Symons works, Bristol Road, Bridgwater, c. 1950. Clay pits, where the alluvial river clay was excavated, were common sights near the River Parrett; upstream and downstream of Bridgwater at this time. Of all the brick and tilemakers in Bridgwater, none was larger and had more dispersed workings than Colthurst Symons and Co. Ltd, with brick and tileyards at Castlefields, Somerset Bridge, Combwich, Puriton and Burnham-on-Sea. (Photographic Collection 1991/60)

Making clay drains at a Colthurst Symons works, *c.* 1951. The Bridgwater brick and tile industry was by this time in terminal decline. With many processes still performed by hand, it was undercut in the 1960s by both the newly formed London Brick Company, which had far lower production costs, and the growing popularity of concrete products. However, some processes were mechanized. Here, Bridgwater MP Gerald Wills watches the making of drains. (GP571)

Derelict brick kilns at the former Barhams Yard, East Quay, Bridgwater, *c.* 1981. One by one the brickyards were run down and closed, the last in 1970. Barham Brothers on East Quay ceased production in 1965. The brickyard sites were gradually converted to light industry. (V509)

Rolling sheet lead at Henry Bell's, Wellington Road, Bridgwater, c. 1957. Metalworking trades had been long established in Bridgwater, making wares to support traditional industries like the shipping, agriculture and the brick and tile industry. Bell's was one of several foundries in the town. Company Director, Horace Bell, is standing at the back of the workshop. (GP12O)

The Somerset Wire Works, Bristol Road, Bridgwater, 1960. This was altogether a larger undertaking. (60121)

33

S. Leffman Ltd, Provident Place, Bridgwater, 1959. The textile industry was also long established in Bridgwater. Leffman's was a major producer of women's lingerie and foundation garments. The company moved to the town from London in 1939 and had a factory in Provident Place. (59301a)

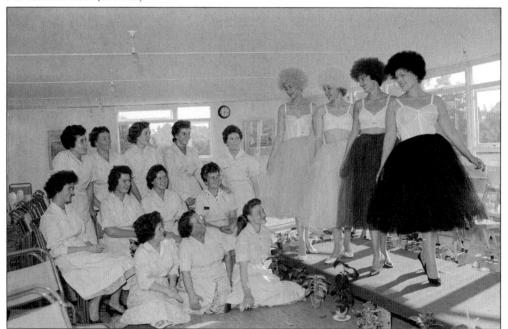

Mannequin parade, S. Leffman Ltd, Provident Place, Bridgwater, 1959. Leffman's specialized in lingerie and was proud to display its wares. This is one of a series of publicity photographs taken by Douglas Allen Photographers in 1959. (59302a)

Making detachable shirt collars, Bridgwater, c. 1955. There were two collar and shirtmaking factories in Bridgwater: Tone Vale Manufacturing (taken over by Van Heusen in 1953) in Bailey Street; and Moody & Co. in New Road. At one time they provided employment for a third of the available female workforce in the town. (GP266)

Marks & Spencer, Cornhill, Bridgwater, 1957. As well as producing their own brand goods, Leffman's became a main supplier of lingerie to Marks & Spencer under the *St Michael* brand. This window display featured not only the product but also a photograph of lingerie production in Bridgwater. (57370a)

Agricultural supplies being unloaded from rail wagons, 1960. Bridgwater, with its docks and railyards, was an important centre for distribution. (60214)

A full quayside at Bridgwater Dock, *c.* 1955. As ships grew larger, this was an increasingly rare sight. The difficult tides and currents of the River Parrett and the tricky entry and exit from Bridgwater Docks meant that fewer ships visited, but there were still times when the docks could seem as busy as in former years. (4715-2)

Unloading at the Bridgwater Warehouse Company, 1959. A variety of bulk goods were unloaded, principally for the agricultural and construction industries. (59146-1)

Unloading goods onto lorries, Bridgwater Docks, 1959. This shipment of bulk goods was clearly part of a large consignment going direct to a purchaser. (59202b)

Bowering's Mill at Bridgwater Docks, 1959. Formerly the Bridgwater Oil and Cake Company, the mill had stood at the end of the Town Dock processing agricultural feeds for more than a century. (59127)

Dunball Wharf, near Bridgwater, 1958. Downstream of the town, bulk goods continued to be landed at Dunball Wharf. J. Bibby & Sons had set up an agricultural feed processing and distribution depot here in 1951. (58225a)

Quantock Preserving Co., Wembdon Road, Bridgwater, 1959. Large boiling-vats at the jam factory were fired by coal. The Quantock Preserving Co. (taken over by Robertson's Jams in 1965) was making jams and preserves as it had done since 1922. (59202-4)

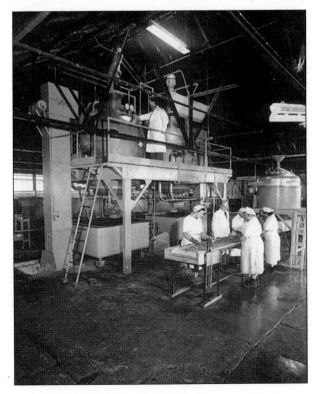

Quantock Preserving Co., Wembdon Road, Bridgwater, 1957. Preparing fruit for jam. The works continued to be an important employer in Bridgwater, even after conversion to the production of fruit juices. (57143)

Bridgwater Docks, 1949. A fishing competition shares space with local steamer Crowpill at Bridgwater Docks. Gradually, the Docks became uneconomic and were surrendered to more leisurely pursuits. They were closed in 1971, although the Port of Bridgwater continues in existence at Dunball Wharf. (GP466)

Four
School Days

Dr Morgan's School Rugby Team, 1953-1954, in April 1954. Dr Morgan's Grammar School for Boys was founded in Bridgwater in 1723. (54183b)

Westover Secondary School, Wembdon Road, Bridgwater, Speech Day, July 1957. Pupils with pets! (57315a)

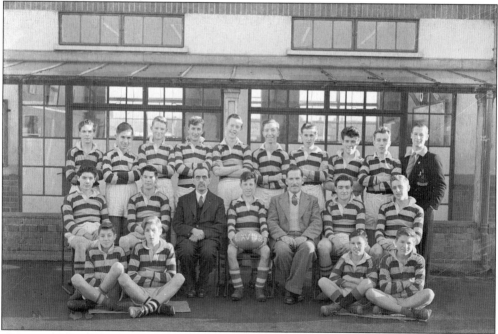

Westover School Rugby Team, 1954-1955. The photograph was taken in November 1955. (56455)

Blake County Secondary School, Bridgwater, March 1957. Students sit engrossed, in their new classroom. The school was officially opened in June 1957 as part of Bridgwater's celebrations for the 300th Anniversary of the death of Robert Blake. (57163a)

Domestic Science class at Blake County Secondary School in March 1957. (57163b)

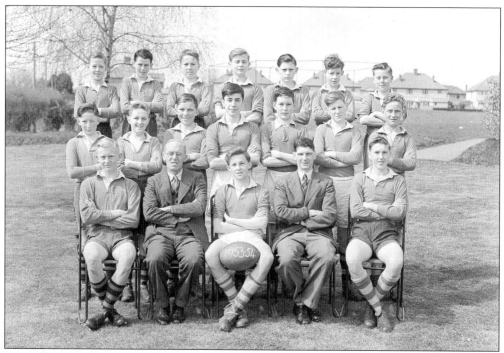

Dr Morgan's School Rugby Team, 1953-1954. This photograph was taken in April 1954. (54183a)

Dr Morgan's School Cricket First XI, 1956. The team is seen here after a record eight undefeated school matches. Sitting in the centre is the captain, S. Berry, and standing on the right is cricket master Mr Colin Uzzell. (56315a)

Bridgwater Girls' Grammar School, Speech Day at Bridgwater Town Hall in November 1954. This was the school's Jubilee year. (54380)

Bridgwater Girls' Grammar School, Park Road, Bridgwater. A garden party was held in the school grounds in July 1955. Pupils put on a display of gymnastics for the visitors. The school moved to this site in 1929. (55267a)

Bridgwater Girls' Grammar School. Girls working hard in the school library in May 1955. (55222)

Dr Morgan's School, Durleigh Road, Bridgwater, 1955. Boys working on the construction of their new swimming pool, under the keen supervision of Headmaster, Mr Charles Key (far right). (55265a)

St Joseph's Roman Catholic School. On 17 March 1954 the school presented 'A Grand Variety Concert' at Bridgwater Town Hall. This photograph may well show some of the cast members in Blake Gardens in February 1954. (54161)

St Margaret's School Sixth Form, October 1955. St Margaret's was an Independent school with sites for juniors at Northfield and seniors at Wembdon Road in Bridgwater. (55367)

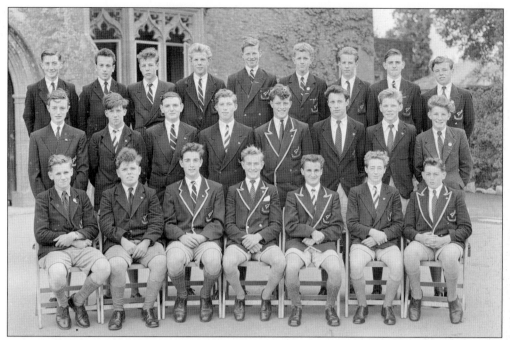

Brymore Secondary Technical School of Agriculture, group photograph at Cannington, June 1957. (57286a)

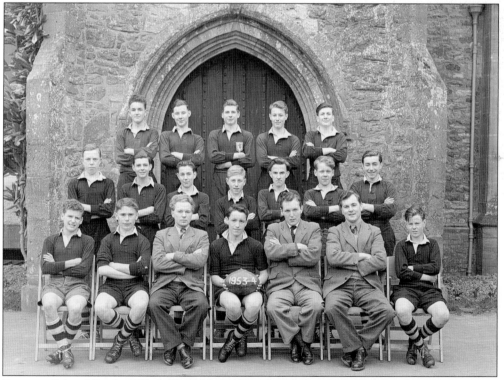

Brymore School Rugby XV, 1953-1954. In their first full season of rugby, the Brymore team won 8 games out of 13. The photograph was taken in April 1954. (54174)

Somerset Farm Institute, Cannington, 1955. The first Speech Day and Prize-giving was held in July 1955. Lord Waldegrave awards Mr P.J. Sweet a travelling clock for achieving the highest marks in the agriculture examination. (55292a)

Somerset Farm Institute, Cannington, 1956. Mr D. Heathcoat Amory, MP presents the second prize for agriculture to Mr E. Joyce of Durleigh Road, Bridgwater at the Institute's Prize-giving in July 1956. (56321a)

Five
Skittles and other Pursuits

The Skittles Team from the Anchor Inn, Combwich, pose for a group photograph in March 1956. As with many West Country communities, skittles continues to be an important sporting pastime in and around Bridgwater. (56223)

The Lime Kiln Ladies' Skittles Team, Bridgwater, May 1956. The team were runners-up in the Bridgwater and District Ladies Skittle League, Knockout Cup, in the 1956 season. Mrs Snook, seated in the centre of the front row, was the popular landlady of the Lime Kiln Inn, which she ran with her husband Jack. (56267)

Blackbirds Men's Skittles Team, 1954. Members of the team were photographed after winning the Western Region All Lines Challenge Cup. Having played matches all over the West Country, the Blackbirds beat Newton Abbot in the final game in May 1954. (54220a)

The Lime Kiln Ladies' Skittles Team, Bridgwater, 1957. The team was photographed enjoying their annual dinner in June 1957. (57265)

The Nondescripts Men's Skittles Team, Bridgwater, 1954. The team posed outside their headquarters, the Bath Bridge Inn, Bath Road, Bridgwater. In April 1954 the Nondescripts became champions in the knockout and overall runners-up in Division III of the Bridgwater Town and District League. (54222)

Bridgwater & Albion Rugby Football Club, 1954. In April 1954 Mr G. Bastable, chairman of Bridgwater and Albion Rugby Football Club, introduced the Mayor of Bridgwater, Mr G.N. Hayball to visiting captain Dr Jack Matthews, of Wales, Barbarians and Cardiff. The highlight of the 1953-1954 season was the visit of Matthews' XV, to Bridgwater. Bridgwater and Albion scored twelve points to the visitor' nineteen. On the left is Mr Hubert Johnston, chairman of Cardiff Rugby Club, and Mr Bastable stands to the rear. (54184a)

The Somerset County Rugby Team, 1955. The team disappointed their fans by losing to Cornwall in October 1955 in front of a record crowd of 5,000 at the Taunton Road ground in Bridgwater. Four players from Bridgwater and Albion RFC played in the match, they were: D. Williams, C. Ball, J. Andrews, and R. Bastable. (55352a)

The Cross Rifles Hotel Men's Skittles Team, Bridgwater, June 1957. (57280a)

The Cross Rifles Hotel Men's Skittles Team, Bridgwater, 1956. The team from the Cross Rifles Hotel, enjoying their annual team outing in June 1956. The landlord of the Cross Rifles, from 1954-1970, was John Peckham. (56274)

The Devonshire Arms Ladies' Skittles Team, Bridgwater, February 1954. The landlord of the Devonshire Arms in St John's Street, from 1948-1957, was Cecil Elvin Hockey. (54151)

The Fleur de Lys Skittles Team, Bridgwater, 1955. In May 1955 a crowd of 200 watched the Fleur de Lys Skittles Team win the Bridgwater Premier Skittles Trophy for the third successive season. (55219)

The Three Crowns Men's Skittles Team, Bridgwater, 1957. The team members were photographed at their annual dinner in May 1957. (57240a)

The Bristol and Exeter Inn Darts Club, Bridgwater, 1955. The team was photographed after winning the Taunton Cyder Trophy in July 1955. (55284a)

The Blue Boar Inn Men's Skittles Team, Bridgwater, May 1958. (58237a)

The Bunch of Grapes Skittles Team, Bridgwater, May1958. The Cross family ran the Bunch of Grapes in St John's Street in the 1950s. (58218a)

Six

All the World's a Stage...

My *Three Angels*, Bridgwater Dramatic Club, 31 October-2 November 1957. The club's autumn show, at Bridgwater Town Hall, was an adaptation of a French play by Albert Husson. The three 'angels' playing convicts in French Guiana were: Richard Forrest; Cyril Epps; and Thomas Edmund. (57407a)

Dick Whittington and his Cat, Bridgwater Branch of the British Legion, January 1954. This pantomime attracted large audiences to Bridgwater Town Hall. The part of Dick Whittington was played by Zita Ashman, with Jean Summers playing the part of Alice. The *Bridgwater Mercury* praised Wally Durant who played Sarah, the cook: 'his droll manner, ridiculous antics and varied expressions enlivened the proceedings.' Other cast members seen here include: Bill Sykes as Idle Jack, Peter Summerhayes as Alderman Fitzwarren, Jack Watt as Captain, Bert Bernard as Mate, Billy Jacobs as King Rat, Jenny Wide as Fairy Queen, Betty Jackson as Tommy the Cat, and Charles Hodgson as the Emperor of Morocco. (54101)

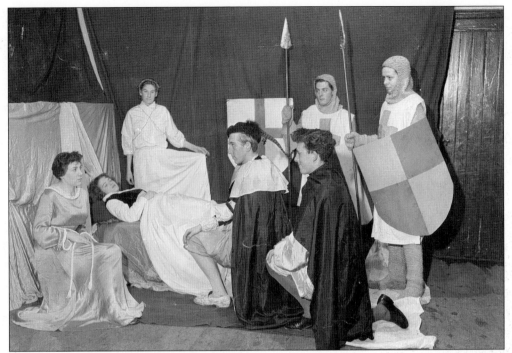

Sleeping Beauty, Spaxton Youth Club, 1956. Amateur drama was one of the most thriving activities in Bridgwater during the 1950s. Not only were there two principal clubs, The Bridgwater Dramatic Society and The Blake Drama Club, there were also school productions, pantomimes, village groups, clubs in factories and productions from the town's own Arts Centre. (56446a)

Robinson Crusoe, Bridgwater Branch of the British Legion, January 1956. The cast at Bridgwater Town Hall included: Joan Barnett as Robinson Crusoe, and Peter Summerhayes as the Dame, with Peter Barnet, Betty Rawlings, Jenny Wide, Fred Thomas, and Muriel Abel. (56101a)

Little Boy Blue, Cranleigh Community Centre, January 1957. The pantomime was written by John Stanley and popular local comedian Bill Jacobs took the role of Mother Hubbard. (57122a)

Mercenary Mary, Bridgwater Operatic Society, 3-8 May 1954. The cast, who performed this musical comedy at Bridgwater Town Hall, included: Robert Parnell, Eddie Hancock, Peter Cunningham, Jean Summers, and Betty Rawlings. (54196a)

The Merry Widow, Bridgwater Amateur Operatic Society, 3-7 March 1959. This production of Franz Lehar's operetta played to packed houses at Bridgwater Town Hall. The can-can dancers, seen here, came from the Bridgwater School of Dancing: Jane Donaldson, Jennifer Graham, Barbara Dodge, Jennifer Horton, Frances Jeal, and Susan Pole. (59121a)

Playboy of the Western World, Bridgwater Arts Players, 14-16 November 1957. The play, by John M. Synge, was performed at Bridgwater Arts Centre. (57418-5)

The Neighbours, The Spaxton Players, 1954. In this photograph, The Players are performing in competition at The Somerset County Drama Festival at Bridgwater Arts Centre in March 1954. Bridgwater hosted regional competitions and drama festivals of both adult and youth theatre. Cast members included: Violet Mounter, Geoffrey Cooks, Dorcas Harris, Queenie Cavill, Alfred Dimond, and Pat Stevens. (54142)

It's Never Too Late, Bridgwater Dramatic Club, 7-9 March 1957. Written by Felicity Douglas, this comedy was about a married woman who finds success as an author. The cast at Bridgwater Town Hall included: Marjorie Pardoe as the lead character, with Clare Bowen, Richard Forrest, Valerie Marks, Derek Holman, and Jean Phillips. (57161a)

You Can't Take It With You, Blake Drama Club, 21-23 November 1957. This was a year of comedy for Bridgwater's amateur dramatic groups. In this production, staged at Bridgwater Town Hall, the setting is New York. The cast received an excellent review and included: Stanley Bollom, Joan Phillips, Billie Bond, Margaret James, and Bernard Storer as members of the Sycamore family. The club won The Phoebe Rees Challenge Trophy for this production. (57421b)

Wild Goose Chase, Blake Drama Club, 19-21 March 1959. The local press reported that this was the club's first attempt at farce. The principal male roles were taken by: Malcolm Davies, Jack Nowell, Ray Worsley, Maurice Vinecombe, and John Gage. The women players were: Lillian Styles, Norma Collard, Patricia Mary Munn, Joan Phillips, and Diana Sandys. (59158)

Romanoff and Juliet, Blake Drama Club, 26-28 November 1959. Peter Ustinov's popular play received an enthusiastic response from the Town Hall audience. The principal players were, as Romanoff and his family: David Hale, John Gage, and Barbara Sants, and as Juliet and her family: Paddy Turner, Raymond Worsely, and Joan Phillips. (59376a)

It's My Opinion, May 1958. This BBC television programme was broadcast from Bridgwater Town Hall. Eight Bridgwater residents were each given one minute to express their views on a 'pet' subject. The photograph shows the programme's producer, Peter Bale, briefing participants before the show. However, there was only time for six to speak and they were: Mr F. Phillips, Bridgwater Labour Party organizer, Mr J. Shaw, from Wilmot Breeden Ltd, Mrs Russell Smith, a teacher at an independent school, Cllr K. Williams, leader of the Bridgwater Labour Group, Mr Metford Jeanes, chairman of the Divisional Conservative Association, and Cllr W.J.B. Staple, a mental-welfare officer. (58212)

St Hilda's School, Nativity Play, Saturday 15 December 1956. Over 100 pupils from the school took part in two performances of their play at Bridgwater Arts Centre. St Hilda's was a girls' boarding school and kindergarten at Otterhampton, near Bridgwater. (56441a)

Good Friday, Monmouth Street Methodist church, Easter 1954. This play, written by John Masefield, was performed on an open stage, across the whole width of the church. The play's producer was Mr Alec Bell, a director of Henry Bell's Engineering in Wellington Road. (54177)

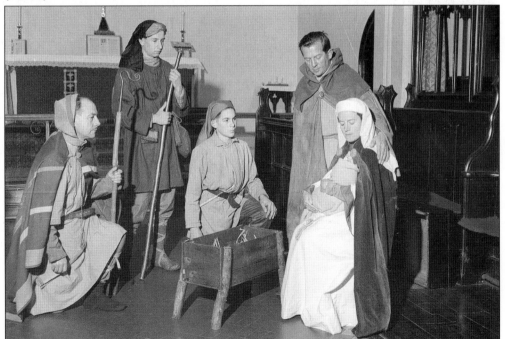

Holy Trinity Church Players, Nativity Play, Friday 20 and Sunday 22 December 1957. (57438a)

Antigone, Bridgwater Girls' Grammar School, April 1954. Sophocles' classic Greek tragedy was performed at Bridgwater Arts Centre. Cast members included: Mary Carpenter, Elizabeth Richards, Meta Hill, Janet Evans, Jane Blay, Suzette Lawrence, and May Bawden. (54160)

Seven

Carnival

Squibbing in High Street, at the annual Bridgwater Guy Fawkes Carnival, *c.* 1950. (V98-10)

Lime Kiln Carnival Club, 1955. Club members pose in their costumes for *The Mississippi Showboat*. (55349f)

The Mississippi Showboat, Lime Kiln Carnival Club, Bridgwater Carnival, Thursday 3 November 1955. Like many contemporary clubs, the Lime Kiln Carnival Club was formed before the Second World War. There were no carnivals held during the war years but this club, along with many others, reformed in 1947. (55377a)

Automation Here We Come, Lime Kiln Carnival Club, 1956. This entry won third place in the Feature Class at Bridgwater Carnival on Thursday 8 November 1956. (56413a)

For Whom The Bell Tolls, Lime Kiln Carnival Club, 1957. The club won first place in the Feature Class at Bridgwater on Thursday 7 November 1957. (57411d)

Golden Lion Carnival Club, 1955. Club members pose as *The Ancient Egyptians*. (55349g)

The Ancient Egyptians, Golden Lion Carnival Club, Bridgwater Carnival, 3 November 1955. The Golden Lion Carnival Club was established in 1937, the Coronation year of George VI, under the original name of the Coronoddies Carnival Club, and had its headquarters at the Lime Kiln Inn. After the Second World War the Club reformed at the Golden Lion Inn under the name of the New Coronoddies Carnival Club and finally changed the name to the Golden Lion Carnival Club in the mid-1950s. (55377b)

Kraft Carnival Club, 1955. Club members pose in their costumes for *The Legend of the Three Princes*. (55349a)

The Legend of the Three Princes, Kraft Carnival Club, Bridgwater Carnival, 3 November 1955. This club was established before the Second World War, and reformed in 1947 with its headquarters at the Olde Oak Inn. In 1948 the club headquarters moved to the Devonshire Arms. (55377c)

Cardiff Arms Carnival Club, 1955. Club members pose in their costumes for *Eastern Fantasies*. (55349b)

Spanish Capers, Cardiff Arms Carnival Club, 1954. This entry came fourth in the Feature Class in 1954. The Cardiff Arms Carnival Club was first formed in 1937 by Harry Crocker and Len Rawles, and reformed in 1947. (54369a)

W & F Wills Carnival Club, 1955. *Carnival Reminiscences – Long Live the Bridgwater Carnival* was the club's contribution to the 350th Anniversary celebration of the Bridgwater Carnival in 1955. (55349c)

Carnival Reminiscences, W & F Wills Carnival Club, Bridgwater Carnival, 3 November 1955. This club was formed in 1953, in response to an appeal by the employees of local engineering firm W & F Wills. The club headquarters were at the Rose and Crown Inn in St Mary's Street. (55377)

Roberts Brothers Carnival Club, 1955. Club members pose in costume for HMS *Carnival*.
(55349d)

HMS *Carnival*, Roberts Brothers Carnival Club, Bridgwater Carnival, 3 November 1955. This
club was formed in 1950 and changed its name to the Revellers Carnival Club in 1959.
(55377e)

Lady Fu Chen Returns, W & F Wills Carnival Club, Bridgwater Carnival, Thursday 6 November 1958. (58359a)

Bustles and Boaters, Roberts Brothers Carnival Club, Bridgwater Carnival, 6 November 1958. The club borrowed the British Flag Carnival Club's trailer for this exhibit. (58359b)

The Red Devils, Hope Inn Carnival Club Bridgwater Carnival, 3 November 1955. The club was formed in 1935 and is reputed to be the oldest carnival club in Bridgwater. (55377f)

Marco Polo, British Flag Carnival Club, Bridgwater Carnival, 3 November 1955. (55377g)

Wee Folk from Holland was presented by *Miss Atyeo and Company* in the Juvenile Feature Class at Bridgwater Carnival on Thursday 4 November 1954. (54369b)

The official opening on the first night of the annual Carnival Concert, 3 October 1955. The event was presided over by the Mayor, Alderman R. Biddescombe, who was supported by the Deputy Mayor, Alderman P. Wills, president Gerald Wills MP, Colin Mackenzie, Alderman E. Wills and councillors C.P. Staple and W.J. Hooper. (55349e)

Eight
Congratulations...

Mr and Mrs Banwell, June 1956. Miss S. Cook and Mr A. Banwell, both from Bridgwater, were married at Holy Trinity church in Taunton Road. The 1950s mark a turning point in the history of weddings. More people of more classes chose to marry in church with a party for family and friends. In fact, the photographs from this period set the scene for the white weddings we recognize today. (56286f)

Mr Haggett, 16 June 1956. The groom, Denis Haggett, arrives at All Saints church, Ashcott with his supporters, brothers Peter (best man) and Rex (usher). (56290v)

Mr and Mrs Seymour, March 1957. The bridesmaids and a pageboy arrive at St Mary's church, Bridgwater for the marriage of Miss G. Hill, of North Petherton to Mr B. Seymour of Bridgwater. (57167b)

Mr and Miss Hindle, 3 August 1957. The bride and her father arrive at St John's church, Pawlett. It became a big tradition in the 1950s for the father of the bride to give his daughter away. Mary Hindle married Bryan Walker, of Yorkshire. (57328b)

St John's church, Bridgwater, 14 July 1956. It was not only members of the bridal party who were kept waiting at the church; these two wedding-car chauffeurs are waiting for Miss D. Dicks and Mr A. Cummings. (56303c)

Mr and Mrs Haggett, 16 June 1956. The marriage of Denis Haggett and Margaret Hawkins took place at All Saints' church, Ashcott. The bride was given away by her brother, Wallace, and wore a dress of net and floral lace decorated with pearls and sequins. The reception was held at Ashcott Memorial Hall, and the honeymoon was spent in Jersey. (56290a)

Mr and Mrs Perry, 2 June 1956. The marriage of Allan Perry and Diana Young took place at St John's church, Bridgwater. The bride was given away by her father and wore a dress of net with matching veil and a flowered headdress. Her bouquet was of pink roses and trailing fern. The reception was held at the New Market Hotel, Bridgwater and the honeymoon was spent at Newquay in Cornwall. (56296a)

St Joseph's church, Bridgwater, 29 August 1957. The marriage of Miss Mitchell and her husband (groom's name unknown) . (57334l)

Mr and Mrs Counsell, 5 October 1957. The marriage of Betty Baldwin and Jack Counsell took place at Durleigh church. The bride was given away by her stepbrother, Eric Gibson, and wore a full-length dress of lace and net. The reception was held at the Blake Arms Hotel, Penel Orlieu, Bridgwater. (57383l)

Mr and Mrs Saunders, 17 October 1959. Friends raise an archway of hatchets for the newly married couple. Miss B. Greenslade and Mr M. Saunders were married at Greenfield (Holy Trinity) church, Hamp in Bridgwater. (59350b)

Mr and Mrs Haggett, 16 June 1956. No wedding was complete without good wishes from onlookers and symbols of good luck and a prosperous future, especially when presented by children. Margaret Haggett (*née* Hawkins) is receiving silver horseshoes from Joyce Boyer and Margaret Blackwood, a lucky black cat from Angela Lockyer and a wooden spoon from Patricia Lockyer. (56290d)

Mr and Mrs Bird, 4 February 1957. A shower of confetti greets the bride and groom at St Mary's church, Bridgwater. (57156f)

Mr and Mrs Pullman, 11 March 1957. More confetti is thrown at St Mary's church, Bridgwater, this time for Susan Jarman of Bridgwater and John Pullman of Woking. (57159o)

Mr and Mrs Fox, 21 March 1957. Gillian Martin, from Westonzoyland, married Sgt Jack Fox, of the RAF, at St Mary's church, Bridgwater. The bride, who worked at Hooper's in Bridgwater High Street, was given away by her brother Peter. The bridesmaids were her sisters, Shirley and Norma and the best man was the groom's brother Robert. The reception was held at Westonzoyland village hall and the honeymoon was spent in Jersey. (57175u)

Mr and Mrs West, 8 September 1956. Doreen Popham, from Cannington and Keith West, from Wembdon, toast the happy occasion with well-wishers outside St Mary's church, Cannington. (56359y)

Mr and Mrs Hill, 5 December 1959. Not everyone wanted a big church affair. Almost a quarter of all weddings were held in register offices during the 1950s. This marriage between Miss Janet Lewis and Mr F.J. Hill, both of Bridgwater, was held at Bridgwater Register Office. (59384c)

Dowdle and Rainier, 9 June 1959. The bride and groom get ready to leave Bridgwater Register Office. (59238e)

Mr and Mrs Dibble, 21 September 1957. The Royal Clarence Hotel in Bridgwater was a popular venue for wedding receptions and provided many opportunities for stylish photographs. Miss Barbara White, of Cannington and Edward Dibble, of Beercrocombe were married at St Joseph's church, Bridgwater. (57369c)

Mr and Mrs Fox, 21 March 1957. The highlight of many wedding receptions is, of course, the best man's speech. Here Robert Fox entertains family and friends at the reception for his brother Jack and bride Gillian at Westonzoyland village hall. (57175p)

Nine
... and Celebrations

Coronation of Queen Elizabeth II, June 1953. Street party for residents of Roseberry Avenue and Bailey Street, one of the many Bridgwater parties held to celebrate the Coronation. (GP34)

Mrs Mouzouri enjoyed her 21st birthday with her husband and family in June 1955. (55268)

Mrs Hartree celebrated reaching the remarkable age of 101 in May 1958. (58231)

Miss Woolridge's 21st birthday in June 1954. The birthday tea with sandwiches, orangeade and beer sits on top of a patriotic Union Flag, which may have been left over from a Coronation party. (54237a)

Mrs Greenslade commemorated her 99th birthday in April 1958. (58206)

Mr and Mrs Emery celebrated their Golden Wedding Anniversary in August 1957. (57333a)

Mr and Mrs George Dennison cutting the cake on their Diamond Wedding Anniversary in May 1955. Mr Dennison is seen wearing a small gold earring in each ear, a memento of his sailing past – his father owned three canal boats in Bridgwater and as an adult Mr Dennison joined the merchant navy. (55201)

Mr and Mrs W.R. Hogarth, parents of seven sons and one daughter, seen here on their Golden Wedding Anniversary in November 1954. Mr Hogarth was one of the first soldiers to win the Military Medal in the Battle of the Somme during the First World War. A week prior to their anniversary the couple learned that they would have to leave their Barclay Street home in Bridgwater because of the new Broadway relief road scheme. (54367)

Mr and Mrs Albert Pyke, together with Ginger the cat, pose for a photograph on their Golden Wedding Anniversary in February 1955. (55130)

Mr Thomas enjoyed his 21st birthday with his family in February 1957. (57131a)

Miss M. Florence's 21st birthday celebrations in April 1957. (57202a)

Mr and Mrs J. Barnett of Cannington, photographed with their son and two daughters on their Golden Wedding Anniversary in July 1956. (56323a)

Mr and Mrs Dyment of Durleigh cut the cake on their Silver Wedding Anniversary in January 1958. (58107)

Mr and Mrs Graham James and family, seen here at the christening of their third child in August 1958. (58307)

Mrs Keil celebrated fifty years as the organist at Middlezoy church in October 1957. (57415a)

Mr and Mrs G.W. Ives, 1957. The whole family enjoyed this Golden Wedding Anniversary in November 1957. (57440-8)

Mr and Mrs G.W. Heywood of Cannington, seen here at their Golden Wedding Anniversary celebrations in January 1957. (57121a)

Mr Chick received a long service award from the Gas Board in May 1957. (57232a)

Mr Gower was presented with a long service award by Mr Edmund Porter, Managing Director of John Browne & Co. Ltd, after fifty years service at the brick and tile manufacturers, in December 1959. (59392a)

Ten
Out and About

Burrow Mump, Burrowbridge, near Bridgwater, September 1984. In the post-war years the beauty of the scenery around Bridgwater became a magnet for tourist and photographer alike. (V608-1)

Sedgemoor Battlefield Memorial, near Westonzoyland. The memorial was unveiled in the 1920s to commemorate those who lost their lives in the last battle on English soil: The Battle of Sedgemoor in July 1685. (V131a)

Summer on the Somerset Levels, near Chedzoy, c. 1951. Idyllic scenes such as these drew the eye of the photographer. Douglas Allen used a *Leica* 35mm camera and a folding *Super Ikonta* for most of his work. (V276-1)

The Quantock Hills, looking towards Merridge Hill. One of England's areas of outstanding natural beauty, this is one of many views taken by Douglas Allen and offered to the *Bridgwater Mercury* as a possible front-page image. (V33-1)

The Bridgwater and Taunton Canal. The canal, which opened to Huntworth in 1827 and to Bridgwater Docks in 1841, was originally planned to be a part of a larger scheme to link the Bristol and English Channels. The project was never finished, for it was rapidly superseded by the railway. (V193)

Looking towards Hinkley Point and across Bridgwater Bay from the Quantock Ridge. Any trip to the Bridgwater area would not be complete without sampling the beauties of the Quantock Hills which, in a relatively small area, provide a range of scenery, like this open heathland. (V110-3)

Holford, near Bridgwater. Picturesque villages on the lower slopes of the Quantocks continue to attract tourists and photographers. (V23-10)

Stolford Flats, near Bridgwater, *c.* 1965. The coastline of Bridgwater Bay has its own particular charm. This view across Stolford Flats features the newly built Hinkley Point power station. (V513)

Cossington railway station, near Bridgwater, *c.* 1951. The Somerset and Dorset branch line to Bridgwater opened in 1890 and closed to passengers in 1952. (564)

Demolition of the rail bridge across Bristol Road, Bridgwater, 1957. The last passenger train for Edington Junction left Bridgwater in 1952 and the line closed to freight traffic in 1954. (57405a)

Bridgwater railway station. Built in 1841 on the Bristol and Exeter line, this was the only main line station left for rail passengers to Bridgwater after the closure of the Somerset and Dorset line. (GP569)

Local enthusiasts seen here before leaving on a treasure hunt, *c.* 1950. The post-war years were to become full of motoring fun, with cars the main means of access to the countryside. (258)

Holford Glen Garage, near Bridgwater, 1955. It was the heyday of the village garage – there was at least one in most villages. (55108)

Bridgwater competitors in the Monte Carlo Rally, 1954. Some motorists were keen to undertake more testing challenges. Standing by the driver's door is local garage owner, Mr Griffiths. (GP573)

Stogursey Motors, Stogursey, near Bridgwater, 1956. Not only would the village garage fix your car, they could also provide heating oil, gas and 'mod-cons' for their local community. (56402a)

Holiday traffic, Bristol Road, Bridgwater, 1955. The increasing use of the motorcar brought traffic jams to Bridgwater. On the day that this photograph was taken, the *Bridgwater Mercury* reported traffic queued back to Dunball. The main route from Bristol to the south-west passed through the town. (55303-5)

Traffic congestion, Town Bridge, Bridgwater, 1955. Until 1957 the Town Bridge was the only crossing point on the lower reaches of the River Parrett. Travelling to or from Taunton or North Devon, there was no way of avoiding congestion in Bridgwater. The opening of the M5 in 1973 took most of the long-distance holiday traffic away from the centre of the town. (55303-1)

The riverside at Combwich, near Bridgwater, c. 1955-65. Combwich, on the lower reaches of the River Parrett, had a small natural harbour and continued to attract coastal craft. Bridgwater coal merchants, Sully and Co. owned the steamer *Crowpill* from 1934-1966. (V22-2)

Hawkridge Reservoir, near Bridgwater, winter 1963. Although the summer tourists had gone the photographer could still be found out and about on the Quantocks with his camera. (V108.3)

Eleven

Country Life

Bridgwater Woolgrowers Ltd, collection and sorting of wool, 1959. Larger and more sophisticated markets meant that the products of the land needed to be carefully collected and graded. (59304)

The Hunt at The Tynte Arms, Enmore, near Bridgwater, c. 1951. The hunt brought together all classes of rural society. (165)

Mr Moore and his horse Ginger. It was easy for the photographer to capture the idyllic side of country life in the post-war years – for it was a time of relative agricultural prosperity; a time when the old ways, still very much in evidence, were about to undergo rapid change. (55142)

The annual Holford pony round up, *c.* 1949. First, catch and train your pony! (V146-1)

Young pony riders on the Quantocks. Horse riding was increasingly a pastime to be learned young, if you had the opportunity. (V522)

Onion sellers, at East Huntspill, c. 1951-1954. For those who had little opportunity to stir far from their country cottage the annual visit of the French and Spanish onion sellers brought variety to the daily routine. (272/543)

J.E. Haggett, Oil Delivery near Chedzoy, c. 1950. The oilman, with his horse and cart, brought paraffin for heating and lighting. Piped gas was rare and electricity was only beginning to spread to the countryside in the post-war years. (223)

Armoury Garage, Friarn Street, Bridgwater with gas dealer, Cyril F. Callow's new vehicle, 1950. Altogether more modern, in his motorvan, was the man who delivered bottled gas. (196)

Out on his ear, near North Newton. Life in the country was not always idyllic or predictable – evictions, especially from tied cottages, were not uncommon. (270)

On the withy beds, near Creech St Michael. The countryside around Bridgwater supported a variety of local industries. On the Somerset Levels, withies – a variety of willow – were seasonally grown and harvested. (V609-5)

Mr Stone, the blind basketmaker from Bawdrip, near Bridgwater. Once processed, the withies were woven into baskets and wicker furniture. (GP239)

Mr A. Gooding cutting and stacking peat near Sharpham. The peat industry was an important part of the rural economy on the Somerset Moors near Bridgwater. (GP302)

Cider-making on a farm in the Woolmersden area, North Petherton, *c*. 1954. Small cider orchards surrounded many local villages and many families made cider on a small scale. This cider press would have been part of a larger production system. (V421)

Annual Ploughing Match, Blackmore Farm, Cannington, 1955. For most people in the countryside it was farming that provided year-round employment. By the 1950s ploughing with horses had been largely superseded by the use of the tractor. (GP576)

Spreading fertilizer by hand from horse and cart, Mr L. Reed, Burrowbridge near Bridgwater, c. 1950. Simple farm tasks were often still performed by hand. (V45)

Horse-drawn seed drill at Tuttons Farm, Spaxton, near Bridgwater, 1950. Although complex agricultural machinery was becoming more common in the post-war years, it required considerable capital investment. Where a traditional implement from a previous era could still serve, it was used. (V35-2)

Hay-making at Rhode Farm, near Bridgwater, *c.* 1951. Although the hay would be cut with a mower it was still common in the post-war years to turn the hay and gather it by hand into traditional hayricks. Soon, the baler would revolutionize the collection and storage of the hay. (GP197)

Jack Chappell at the wheel of his traction engine, Cokerhust Farm, Wembdon, near Bridgwater, 1957. To assist with harvesting both hay and corn an agricultural contractor might be hired. Traction engines, which had been used for many years, could drive a variety of machinery with moving belts. Tractors, which were replacing them, were originally fitted with pulleys and belts. (57378-2)

Combine harvesters at work, near Cannington, c. 1950. The economic forces that were to revolutionize the British farming industry in the post-war years are to be seen in this cornfield. Not only was farming becoming more mechanized and less labour intensive, it was also becoming more of a large-scale operation. (24)

Hay wain, near Goathurst, *c.* 1950. Horses served as well as tractors to pull the carts that brought in the hay harvest. (V496)